Cross-Country
Ski Conditioning
For Exercise Skiers
and Citizen Racers

Bob Woodward

Contemporary Books, Inc.
Chicago

Library of Congress Cataloging in Publication Data

Woodward, Bob, 1939–
    Cross-country ski conditioning.

    Includes index.
    1. Cross-country skiing   2. Physical fitness.
3. Physical education and training   I. Title.
GV855.3.W66   1981   796.93   81-65177
ISBN 0-8092-5925-7   AACR2
ISBN 0-8092-5924-9 (pbk.)

All photos by Bob Woodward except as otherwise credited.

Copyright © 1981 by Bob Woodward
All rights reserved
Published by Contemporary Books, Inc.
180 North Michigan Avenue, Chicago, Illinois 60601
Manufactured in the United States of America
Library of Congress Catalog Card Number: 81-65177
International Standard Book Number: 0-8092-5925-7 (cloth)
                                    0-8092-5924-9 (paper)

Published simultaneously in Canada by
Beaverbooks, Ltd.
150 Lesmill Road
Don Mills, Ontario M3B 2T5
Canada

To Dave Prokop, the great one, who urged me to write more about skiing. With special thanks to Chuck Bradwell, Paul Daly, Dr. Stan James, Bert Kleerup, and Casey Sheahan.

Contents

Introduction

Cross-country skiing is the fastest-growing participant winter sport in the United States. A decade ago there were less than half a million skiers nationwide. Today there are close to 7 million. Ten years ago most cross-country skiers were hikers and backpackers looking for winter recreation. Today cross-country skiing attracts people from a wide variety of backgrounds and interests who like the sport because it is healthful exercise.

Cross-country skiing has few peers when it comes to total body exercise. The sport strengthens your upper and lower body and your cardiovascular system. At the same time, few sports are as safe: you can cross-country ski for hours without falling victim to the crippling injuries so common in sports done on hard surfaces.

Skiing for exercise takes many forms. Just as a jogger starts out slowly before progressing to running, cross-country skiers generally start as ski tourers before becoming exercise skiers or citizen racers. The big hurdle between tour skiing and citizen racing is learning how to train, or condition.

Note that throughout this book, the terms *training* and *conditioning* are used interchangeably.

Cross-country ski training is easy when you're young. If you are in college or working part-time, there is plenty of time to devote to becoming fit. When you're older, holding down a full-time job and raising a family, finding the time to train is often impossible. It is difficult to train after a long day at work, either because of mental fatigue or because of other obligations.

If the logistical problems of training don't get the working person down, most of the training literature will. The authoritative books on cross-country ski training are written for people who aspire to be the best, to participate on the international level. Very little, if anything, is directed at the person who holds down a nine-to-five job yet would like to train to become a better cross-country skier.

This book was written for the nine-to-fiver. It is intended for the ski tourer, the exercise skier, and the citizen racer who wants to improve his or her physical fitness level while preparing for skiing.

I have taken what I call a "total sport" approach in this book. My goal is to get you out training first with improved cross-country skiing as a bonus. This is a bit contrary to the current philosophy, which says that if you want to do better in cross-country skiing you should work on only those exercises that apply exclusively to the sport. I feel this limits your experience and takes the spice out of training. The spice is variety and fun. If you pick up a fun sport and use it to train your body for cross-country skiing, so much the better. Leave the specific training to the experts; that's part of their job. Have fun and let your training open you up to a variety of athletic activities. If, as a part-time trainer, you become too serious and too specific, you will lose sight of your purpose of becoming a better person through training.

I have also tried to avoid becoming overly technical. While medical, physiological, and biomechanical terminology adds an aura of mystery to a sport, it is often very confusing and can be used to beg or brush over an important question or issue. If we keep it simple, we're on the right track. There are no secrets to training. There are no magic formulas. Training is simply a matter of putting in the time and seeing what the physical and mental results are.

I hope that, after reading this book, you will select a manageable training schedule and stick to it. Make your training fun and enjoyable. Think of it as training for life, not just for skiing. Every hour you spend getting into shape will soon be transformed into days of increased personal enjoyment at work and at play.

1

Getting Ready

Making Time

If you are a working person, the most difficult task you face is blocking out enough time during the day to condition. It is important to make time for conditioning and to try and stick to a regular schedule. This doesn't mean you should get into a boring training rut. It means creating a regular schedule of varied activities.

For working people conditioning three hours a day is impossible. Strive to put in at least a half hour to an hour per day. This is usually easier to do in the spring and summer months when days are longer and the weather is better. With a base of training built over an April-through-November period, all you have to do in the winter is light maintenance training and, of course, lots of skiing.

There Are No Classes

Current cross-country training philosophy places a heavy emphasis on specific training. One noted coach even goes as far as to classify exercises into class one and class two groups. He feels that if you are doing any nonspecific exercising (class two), you are not training properly for cross-country skiing. This, he indicates, is true of the top competitor as well as the person who only has a half hour a day to train.

This is hogwash. While I agree that specificity in training is important for the top competitor and for the weekend skier who wants to emulate the top skiers, it is not as important for most exercise skiers, ski tourers, and citizen racers. If we follow the coach's advice and train specifically, we have to, according to his classifications, give up running, swimming, bicycling, hiking, and kayaking. That would leave most of us with sterile, boring training programs. Let's not shoot for the moon with training programs that have little latitude. Let's enjoy the training process with variety.

Dry-land training creates the conditioning base for skiing.

It All Begins in Spring

The best way to condition for any sport is on a year-round basis. The best athletes don't stop their training after their season is over. They continue to train at varying levels of intensity during the off-season and start a progressive training buildup as the competitive season approaches.

The best way to train for cross-country skiing is to start a conditioning program in the spring, following the end of the ski season, and carry it through until late November, just before the next ski season starts. During this period you will be able to build a base of conditioning that will carry you through the entire ski season. With a solid base of conditioning, winter workouts become low-key maintenance workouts during the week with weekends of skiing.

The sole purpose of dry-land training is to put together the cardiovascular (heart/lungs) and muscular elements that will enhance your skiing days. Cross-country places demands on the cardiovascular system, the upper body, and the lower body, and therefore all three areas have to be trained. Our spring-through-fall dry-land program starts with general training and becomes more specific as the season approaches. Our goal is to become ready for increased activity first, adding specifics that will be directly beneficial to cross-country ski technique later.

Hard/Easy

The key to training for exercise skiing and citizen racing is to create a varied, fun program. If you tackle a hard day-by-day program meant for top international racers, you will soon end up bored or sick. There have been numerous cases of people combining too much office work with hard workouts and becoming mentally and physically exhausted. Overtraining the mind and body can be dangerous.

Variety in training means going hard one day and easy the next. It means doing activities that are good for you, which at the same time are fun. It means taking a rest when you are injured or mentally tired of the strain. It means listening to your body and letting it tell you how it feels.

Hold Back

One of the key elements in training for cross-country skiing is knowing when to push hard and when to hold back. There are lots of stories about top international skiers who are super off-season trainers but who just can't quite get through the ski season without becoming mentally fatigued and physically broken down. Their problem is overtraining.

Overtraining is just as bad as not training at all. I have a friend I call Mrs. Compulsive. As a teacher, her summer days are free and her daily training schedule includes an hour-long run, a bike ride, some tennis, and swimming. Her constant complaint is that she cannot better her times at certain running distances and that she is injury prone. Without rest, her body is unable to go any faster and it breaks down more easily.

Another friend trains like an Olympian: he pushes until he can go no farther. His results are varied. One winter he skis poorly without much zip; the next winter he is sick most of the time. The cause is overtraining.

Now, both these people are what I call *hard-core trainers*. They work at training. But you don't have to be hard-core to fall victim to overtraining. You may have a low-key program, but if you overdo that program and get bored or work out when work at the office and emotional problems become bothersome, you can fall into a slump similar to that experienced by the overtrainer.

Bill Bowerman, the great University of Oregon and Olympic team track coach put it well with his "train, don't strain" philosophy. If you want to have a great winter of exercise skiing and citizen racing, build a solid training program. Try to be less compulsive, if you tend to go overboard in everything you do. Look at the spring and summer months as a time to get ready for skiing, not as a time to grind yourself into the ground with overwork.

2

Cardiovascular Training

The first and most important step in a basic fitness and cross-country ski training program is building cardiovascular endurance and strength. Cross-country skiing is demanding on the heart and lungs, and they must be well conditioned. Since the entire body is active in cross-country ski technique, the cardiovascular system works doubly hard transporting blood to all parts of the body.

The cardiovascular system must be trained in several ways: first, for prolonged activity; second, for prolonged activity interspersed with sudden short bursts of high activity; and third, for short hard bursts of activity.

There are many ways in which you can develop off-season cardiovascular strength. Running is perhaps the most popular form of cardiovascular training because it is easiest to do. Bicycling is excellent for those who suffer from running's pounding. Stationary cycling on an ergometer is perfect for people who dislike running and bicycling.

If you decide to take up one of these three forms of cardiovascular training, or one of the ones we will discuss later, be sure to consult a physician before undertaking a conditioning program. Your physician can recommend levels of training intensity that will best suit your current physical condition. If you are over forty and just starting to train, be sure to get a stress EKG test before undertaking any strenuous activity.

As your training program progresses, check back with your doctor or local fitness clinic to get an update on your progress and to determine whether or not you can increase your activity load.

Running

Running has become a tremendously popular participant sport. While I would rather see people running than riding in cars, I think the running shoe companies should include the following warning on each box of shoes they sell: Caution—running can be hazardous to your feet and legs.

Running is tremendous exercise, but it can be painful if you run on pavement every day. The best running training for cross-country skiing is done off the paved roads. Less time on

Spending less time on the pavement and more on wooded trails is a good rule for running.

the pavement and more time on wooded trails and dirt roads is a good rule of thumb for running in cross-country ski training.

You should concern yourself with four types of runs: long slow distance (LSD), natural intervals, pure intervals, and fartlek. Long slow distance runs are, as the name implies, done over longer distance at a slower pace. The LSD run is good for building a base of cardiovascular endurance. How long and how slow you run depends on the level of training you have achieved. If you are new to running, two miles at ten minutes per mile might be ideal. If you are an intermediate level runner, six to eight miles at a nine-minute-per-mile pace might be perfect. As an experienced, well-trained runner, eight to ten miles at a seven-minute-per-mile pace would be reasonable. By setting a pace and sticking to it over the length of your run, you begin to build the ability of your heart and lungs to work at a higher level of efficiency over a longer period of time.

Natural interval runs respond to terrain changes. You run a course as you would ski it: pacing on the flats, pushing as hard as possible on the uphills, and resting on the downhills. The natural interval run helps your cardiovascular system become accustomed to the sudden hard intervals of work on the uphill, followed by the interval of rest on the downhill and the interval of moderately intense work on the flats. Each interval, or block, of activity is done at a different level of intensity. This is unlike the LSD run, which is done at the same level of intensity for the duration of the workout.

You can run a natural interval run on a hilly section of paved road, but head to the woods for the best results. Running on a wooded trail or an old logging road is mentally stimulating and more like being on a cross-country ski course.

In your natural interval run, be sure to push through the top of the hill. Don't stop at the crest of the hill, rest, and then start running again. Push through the top and then lope down the other side, recovering as you go. This is important for two reasons: first, it teaches you to maintain your momentum through the tops of hills; second, it helps your muscles develop the ability to work anaerobically. Both are very important aspects of cross-country ski training.

Aerobic and Anaerobic Running

Distance running is an aerobic sport. The muscles work aerobically (with oxygen). Aerobic strength comes with cardiovascular training. A trained cardiovascular system takes in and transports oxygen better than an untrained system.

In natural and pure interval runs you begin to force your muscles to work without oxygen. You have probably run up a hill at a quick pace only to feel a sudden burning sensation in your muscles. The burning sensation is the result of the muscles working anaerobically (without oxygen). The sudden explosive action of hill running has exceeded the cardiovascular system's ability to supply sufficient oxygen to all parts of the body. The muscles literally go into oxygen debt. To continue running up the hill, you have to rely on the ability of your muscles to work anaerobically.

Recent tests have shown that most cross-country racers rely on aerobic strength during the initial stages of a hill climb, but as they get near the top of the hill their muscles begin to work anaerobically. Taking this information, you can see why it is so

(Left) The pure interval run develops both aerobic and anaerobic capacities.
(Right) Pure interval runs are best done on a track.

important to run through the top of a hill when your leg muscles are burning and your lungs feel as if they are going to collapse. By running through the top, you are training your muscles to work without oxygen for a short period of time.

Pure Intervals

Pure interval workouts are the best way to develop anaerobic strength in your legs. A pure interval run is best done in a controlled environment, such as a running track, where the length of the run, the rest interval, and the pulse rates are easily monitored. The object of the pure interval workout is to run at or near full speed for a short distance, then jog or walk for a short distance until your heart rate drops back to normal. The duration of the pause between intervals should be no less than thirty seconds and no more than ninety seconds. During this period your heart rate should drop below 120 beats per minute.

When you start your repeat sprints, do them at three-quarter speed. When your heart rate fails to drop below 120/minute during recovery, end the workout.

Top skiers and runners do their intervals on the running track. I often try to find a secluded spot, measure off a set course on a road or path, and run it for my pure interval workout. Gently sloping hill runs are my favorite. Friends who live near the coast or at lakes with sandy beaches swear by pure interval runs in the sand.

Fartlek

Another running option is the fartlek run. Developed by Gustav Holmer of Sweden, the term *fartlek* literally means *speed play*. A fartlek run contains elements of interval training. The object is to run or jog along easily for a while and then push your heart rate way up with a hard effort. After the push, you return to an easy run or jog pace, during which you recover.

The intervals of speed work in a fartlek run vary in distance and intensity. They are spontaneous bursts that take place when the spirit moves you to action. The fun aspect of fartlek is making a game out of the run, sprinting here and there as the terrain or moment dictates.

An important note: *Remember to establish a good aerobic base with steady distance running before attempting interval training.*

Heart Rates

Before we go any further with cardiovascular conditioning, let's discuss the importance of heart rates. Heart rates indicate the condition you are in and should be used during training to monitor your performance.

There are three heart rates that you should be familar with before setting out on a training program: resting rate, maximum rate, and training rate. You have to establish your maximum heart rate and your resting heart rate before you can establish your training rate.

Checking your heart rate during training is the best way to gauge your performance.

Here is a step-by-step procedure for figuring out your heart rates:

1. Just as you awake one morning, place the index and middle fingers of one hand on either your wrist or the carotid artery on your neck and count your pulse for thirty seconds. Multiply the number of beats by two to get your resting pulse.

Example: 30 beats × 2 = 60 per minute = resting pulse

2. Take 220 if you are male and 225 if you are female and subtract your age from this figure to get your maximum pulse rate. Two hundred twenty and 225 are the heart rates of a male baby and a female baby, respectively. By subtraction we get an estimate of our maximum heart rate. A person's maximum heart rate drops with age.

(200 or 225) − age = maximum pulse rate

3. To establish your training heart rate, use the following formula:

[maximum rate (200 or 225) − age − resting pulse] × 65% + resting pulse = training rate

The training rate is the rate at which you get most cardio-vascular conditioning effect. Your cardiovascular workout is affecting you positively if you are working at or above your training rate.

4. To get a range of intensity for workouts, take 60 percent and 90 percent of your maximum heart rate. Train with your heart rate between these two points during most of your workouts.

Here is my own heart rate profile:

resting pulse = 40 per minute
age = 40 years
maximum pulse rate = 180 per minute (220−40)
training heart rate = [180 − 40 (resting pulse)] × 65 percent + 40 (resting pulse) = 131

As soon as I get to 131 beats per minute in a workout, I am improving my cardiovascular conditioning.

Using the formula for range of intensity (60 percent to 90 percent), I find my training range to be between 108 and 162 per minute.

Weight watchers take note: *Fat metabolizes easier at the lower end of your training rate. If losing weight is important to you, work at the low end of your training rate.*

Now, let's apply our heart rate information to the runs we have discussed for cardiovascular conditioning. On an LSD run, your heart rate should hover near your training rate or just below it. If you are new to running and LSD runs, stop every so often and take your pulse. After a few months of training you will begin to know when you are running too slowly and when you are overdoing it during an LSD run.

On a natural interval run, your heart rate will shoot up to near maximum, hover around the training rate, and may fall way below it at times. Let's say you are running along at a steady pace (training rate) and you come to a steep hill in the course. Run the hill and check your pulse rate at the top before proceeding down it. Jog down the hill and recheck your pulse at the bottom. If your pulse is still high, you need more interval work to train your system to accept the sudden bursts of speed in your interval run. If, however, your heart rate has dropped back to the training level, you are getting into shape.

Top athletes like to have their pulse rates return to training level within thirty seconds of the end of an intense interval. Exercise skiers and citizen racers should aim for a sixty-second recovery period.

Earlier we talked about the importance of the recovery period between pure intervals. On every sprint you will push your heart rate to near maximum. After you jog a bit your heart rate should come back to below 120 to give your system full recovery. As we mentioned earlier, when your heart rate fails to drop back to below 120 during your recovery period, it is time to terminate the workout. By continuing after your pulse rate fails to drop, you are losing any training effect and pushing your system too hard.

An important note about heart rates: Many top athletes

check their pulse periodically during the day to gauge their feelings and prepare for the day's training. Stress, fatigue, and the onset of a cold often show up in an inordinately high pulse rate. On high pulse rate days, many top athletes take time off or do a short easy workout.

To gain complete knowledge of your heart rates and the ranges of work best suited to your cardiovascular conditioning, contact a reputable cardiologist or one of the many fine sports medicine clinics springing up around the country. Knowing your heart well is the key to learning how to listen to your body.

Other Cardiovascular Workouts

Ski Walking

Walking and a particular cross-country derivation called ski walking are fine cardiovascular conditioners. Anytime you walk someplace instead of driving, you are doing your heart and lungs a favor.

The ski walk is an exaggerated uphill walk that closely duplicates uphill ski techniques. It is a great way to go up hills when you are out on a hike or when you can't make it to the top of a hill while running.

In the ski walk you step up the hill as far as you can with one leg while reaching up the hill with the opposite arm. The effect is a cross between the Groucho Marx walk and late 1930s Fascist marching. Keep your head up and your eyes focused fifteen to twenty feet ahead on the trail or road. The basic body position and arm and leg movements will carry over directly into your on-snow ski technique.

Hiking

Hiking is a pleasant way to spend a day while getting in some training. Many top skiers use hikes on their easy training day. Hiking over a beautiful trail with friends can be mentally stimulating and, as we often find, physically exhausting.

In the past few years many top skiers have extended their hiking experience by adding speed. Speed hiking is hiking at a quick tempo throughout the length of a hike. It's not running. It's not jogging. It's steady hiking at a fast pace that keeps the heart rate up and makes the muscles work.

Bicycling

Here's a great form of exercise for those who hate the pounding of running. From my own experience, it takes up to three times the distance to get the same training effect on a bicycle as you would in a run. Bicycling's softness on the feet and legs, however, makes it an attractive sport. Bicycling is becoming more important in our lives as energy supplies dwin-

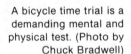

A bicycle time trial is a demanding mental and physical test. (Photo by Chuck Bradwell)

dle, and it is certainly a good way to get in some training while commuting to work or going shopping.

A program of bicycle training could include long slow rides—natural interval rides and intervals. Most rides tend to be natural interval rides unless you live in flat country where you can ride for miles at a steady speed. Recently I tried bicycle time trial racing, which is essentially one long interval. It's man-against-the-clock racing over a set distance.

Time trialing is a good way to push yourself up to the threshold of anaerobic activity and to sustain this level of activity for some length of time. If there are no formal time trials in your area, go out and time yourself over a course. Try to improve your time and learn to push as hard as you can over whatever distance you have chosen. Learning to push when it hurts is valuable training for those who are considering cross-country citizen racing.

On the fun side, bicycle touring is a fine blend of recreational sight-seeing and training. Bicycle touring has become as popular as backpacking and is another way to condition your muscles and cardiovascular systems.

Stationary Cycling

Until recently, most Americans have thought of stationary bicycles as devices designed for use by overweight ladies at Arizona and California fat farms. For years the Finns and Swedes have used stationary bicycles for training. A half-hour workout on a stationary bicycle will make you a believer in their ability to help a person's cardiovascular conditioning.

Stationary bicycles work on resistance. By simply adjusting a knob on the handlebars, the rider can increase or decrease the resistance on the weighted front flywheel. Some models of stationary bicycles, like the Tunturi ergometer, have resistance gauges, speedometers, and timers to help the rider accomplish specific workout requirements.

A typical workout might involve pedaling against a certain amount of resistance at a set speed for a set period of time.

Ergometers are excellent devices for cardiovascular conditioning.

With a low amount of resistance, this workout would be similar to an LSD run.

Another workout might be a progressive one, in which the rider starts out working at low resistance and increases the resistance every three minutes. This workout helps the cardio-vascular system learn to function under increased work loads. The workout also simulates a typical cross-country race for many citizen racers. They start slowly, building up their speed until they arrive at the finish line near exhaustion. Terminate this type of workout when either your heart and lungs won't go on or your muscles begin to tire and burn.

A third stationary bicycle routine is a simple interval work-out. You start by pedaling easily at low resistance. After two minutes, push the resistance up to a level at which you have to work hard, then pump as hard as you can for up to thirty seconds. Following the hard output, reduce the resistance and pedal easily until your pulse rate dips below 120 before doing another repetition.

The beauty of the stationary bicycle is that it can be ridden at home. It's the perfect device for rainy day training. Listen to music, watch television, or read while you pedal; these activities will help take the boredom out of the ride.

Swimming

Swimming is an excellent cardiovascular conditioner and upper body conditioner. I like to swim to limber up the muscles and joints that have become stiff and cramped from other exercises. Swimming laps at the local pool during the winter is fine, but in the summer try to do your swimming outdoors in a lake, river, or ocean to keep the exercise enjoyable.

3

Muscular Conditioning

Cardiovascular conditioning has to be combined with a program of muscular conditioning to complete the cross-country fitness picture. The entire body gets into the act of cross-country skiing and it should be trained to be able to work for longer periods of time without fatigue. If you are running and cycling for cardiovascular conditioning, your lower body muscles will get stronger. Our main concern then is with building your upper body, particularly the shoulder girdle muscles that are so important in poling.

As an exercise skier or citizen racer, your goal should be to develop muscle endurance along with muscle strength. Since most people reach their physical peak in early adulthood, it is important not to get too carried away with a strength program. I issue this admonition so that you won't rush out and try to build a lot of bulky "show" muscles when what you need are "do" muscles.

The Load Carriers

In every sport, certain muscle groups do most of the work.

Since cross-country is a total-body sport, practically every muscle group in the upper and lower body comes into play as you ski. As we describe various exercise routines, we will refer to the specific muscle groups that are important to cross-country skiing. Here is a brief resume of the more important muscle groups and what part they play in ski technique:

Shoulder Girdle Group

"Lats" (*latissimus dorsi*): the muscles that extend from below the shoulder area down the side of the upper torso—very important in poling.

"Delts" (*deltoids*): shoulder muscles at the top of the arm—important in poling.

"Traps" (*trapezius*): muscles extending down from the neck into the upper back and shoulders—important in poling.

"Triceps" (*triceps*): the muscles on the back side of your upper arm—important in poling.

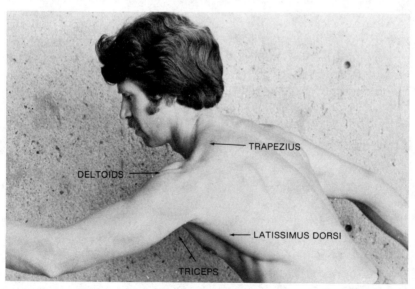

Upper body development is important for cross-country skiing.

Abdominals and Lower Back

"Abs" (*abdominals*): support the upper trunk and are important in trunk bending during double poling.

Lower back muscles (*erector spinae inter spinales*): important trunk support.

Leg Muscles

"Quads" (*quadriceps*): muscles on the front of the thigh—important in the diagonal stride, downhill skiing, turning, and uphill technique.

"Calves" (*gastrocnemius*): important in the diagonal stride and uphill technique.

"Hamstring" (*bicep femoris/semitendinosus/semimembranosus/gracilis/sartorius*): muscles on the back of the thigh—important in the diagonal stride and uphill technique.

Sports Activities for Muscle Tone

There are certain spring-through-fall outdoor sports that are fun to participate in and also work on muscle groups that are important to cross-country skiing. If working on weight machines doesn't appeal to you, stick with a fun outdoor sport to help develop muscle strength and endurance.

Canoeing

You don't have to take an epic two or three-week trip in Minnesota's Boundary Waters Canoe Area to get some muscular benefit from canoeing. An hour of paddling on a local pond, lake, or river is plenty. Canoeing is particularly beneficial to developing shoulder girdle muscles and the abdominals.

There are many forms of canoeing, from flat-water paddling to white-water river running and lazy river touring. Canoeing can be done alone, with a partner, or with the family. It is good natural conditioner for the upper body.

Kayaking

White-water paddling is an excellent upper body developer. It requires strength and draft maneuvering. Less exciting, but equally as good a conditioner, is flat-water kayaking. Virtually unknown in the United States, competitive flat-water paddling is an arduous sport. It requires total concentration and energy output for up to 1,000 meters.

On the noncompetitive level, flat-water kayaking is a wonderful way to see lakes and sections of rivers. You can use a standard white-water kayak for flat-water paddling, but for the best results use a specially designed flat-water boat that cuts the water cleanly and tracks in a straight line.

Flat-water kayaking is a good upper body builder.

An interesting sidelight to kayaking is that there are more kayakers than runners who have become fine cross-country skiers. It has always been thought that runners would provide the nucleus from which better cross-country skiers would emerge. While most runners have well-trained cardiovascular systems, they lack the upper body strength needed to excel in cross-country skiing. Kayakers, on the other hand, seem to be able to train their legs and cardiovascular system well enough to blend in with their superior upper body strength to become top skiers.

Doug Peterson, a member of the U.S. cross-country team, is a good example of a kayaker turned skier. Doug was a member of the U.S. national kayak team before becoming a top skier. On the citizen racer level, Leslie Klein Kearney, top international flat-water and white-water kayak competitor, is a fine skier. Prolific cross-country ski writer Eric Evans was national slalom kayak champion for ten years before establishing himself as a fine cross-country racer.

Rowing

Rowing is excellent for total body development. Done on a grass roots level, rowing can be anything from trolling for trout to taking your sweetie out on the lake for a moonlight cruise. On a more sophisticated level, it is rowing a shell with a sliding seat. Unfortunately, high-level rowing is either restricted to a few universities and coastal towns or is too costly to attract many participants. If you have access to a community crew program, make use of it. High-level rowing is a superior total body conditioner.

Chopping Wood

A few years ago chopping wood was passed off as a New England custom. As sure as sugarin' came in the spring, cuttin' and splittin' wood came in the late summer and fall. Then OPEC raised oil prices and wood gathering became a national pastime as people began to use wood stoves for heating and cooking.

And what a great way to get your upper body in shape for

winter. Hoisting an eight-pound maul over your head several hundred times during a splitting session is tough work and helps build muscle strength and endurance. Wood chopping is a subtle form of training. You become so intent on the end product (wood for heat) that you tend to overlook the physical energy you are putting into the project.

Bouldering: a good example of a fun form of summer training.

Bouldering

Bouldering is rock climbing on local rock outcrops and crags without ropes, hardware, and long vertical drops. Bouldering is mentally challenging and tests upper body strengtth.

Other Sports

Sports like golf, tennis, and racquetball have few muscular benefits for cross-country skiing. If you are interested in developing natural strength and endurance for cross-country skiing, stick with outdoor sports that will work on complementary muscle groups.

In the Gym

Today people have access to either freestanding weights or weight machines at health clubs, schools, or at home. Weight workouts help develop muscular endurance and strength. A good weight workout can be done during a relatively short period of time, making it ideal for days when your schedule is tight.

When working with weights, try to go through your weight routine twice a week. One weight workout per week will only leave you with sore muscles, not the strength and endurance you desire. It is best to alternate workouts. For one workout, use heavier weights with few repetitions of each exercise; on the next workout, use lighter weights and make more repetitions of each exercise. This alternating routine helps build the strength and endurance you will want for cross-country skiing.

Be sure to set down a lifting routine and repeat it twice during your workouts. If you have eight lifts and exercises that make up your routine and each takes two minutes to complete, that's sixteen minutes for one set. Take a rest or a short jog after the first weight/exercise set and then go through each individual routine again to cap a thirty-five- to forty-minute workout.

Universal Gyms

The most readily available weight apparatus for most people is the Universal Gym. A typical Universal Gym setup consists of a cluster of weights surrounded by stations at which you perform lifts or exercises. The amount of weight you work with is established by setting a locking pin into a stack of weights at a desired weight level.

Universal Gyms are not only weight machines; they also have exercise stations. For cross-country ski conditioning, it's best to mix in several exercises with your weight lifts. With the following eight-exercise Universal plan, be sure to note the number of exercise repetitions and the amount of weight you use. These figures become the standards for ensuing workouts and basis against which to measure your progress.

Bench Press: The bench press helps strengthen your chest (pectoral) muscles and triceps. In the photo you will notice that there are two positions for doing this exercise. The second position is normal; the first is best for people who have lower-back problems.

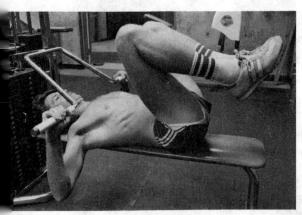

(Left) Step one of the bench press. People with bad backs use the leg position shown.

(Right) Step two of the bench press, showing the normal leg position.

Remember the alternating workout theory. Use heavier weights and make few repetitions of the lift in one workout. During the next workout, use lighter weights and make more repetitions of each lift.

Incline Sit-ups: Most Universal Gyms have an incline sit-up board. Be sure to keep your knees bent. Place your hands behind your head with your elbows flared out, or place them on your chest. Place the board at an angle that allows you to do fifteen to twenty sit-ups before you tire. If you want to put some extra oomph into this exercise, alternate touching the opposite elbow to the opposite knee. Incline sit-ups work on the abdominal muscles.

Back Raisers: You should always balance an exercise on one set of muscles with an exercise on the complementary set of muscles. Immediately after working on your abdominal muscles with incline sit-ups, work on your lower back muscles with back raisers.

Incline sit-ups.

Part one of the back raiser.

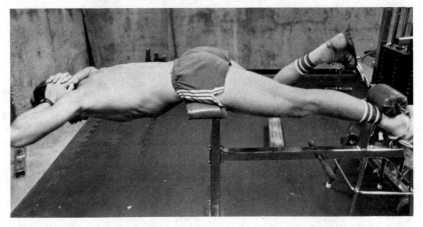

Part two of the back raiser. Do not rise above the horizontal plane.

It's best to keep your elbows flared out well to the side during this exercise. Try not to rise above the horizontal plane on each upward lift. Raising your body too high can be harmful to your back.

Lat Pulls: Because of the importance of the shoulder girdle muscles in poling, they have to be conditioned. You will notice in the photo that the exerciser is using a towel around the bar. Using a towel makes the exercise motion closer to the cross-country ski poling motion.

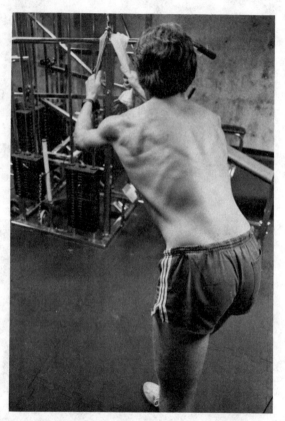

Lat pulls. For best results use a towel wrapped around the pulling bar.

Crushers: I'm sure this is an unofficial name for the exercise, but it graphically expresses how this exercise can feel. The exerciser in the photo uses a weight bar to span the gap in the forked Universal Gym bar. This allows more weight to rest on his shoulders.

Calf crushers.

The two-by-four under the exerciser's toes is very important. You place your toes on the board, rise up as high as you can, then dip back down until your heels are below the board. Do these raises slowly and feel the calf muscles working.

Leg Extensions: In *front,* leg extensions are excellent for strengthening the thighs (quadraceps). A common sight in gymnasiums is an exerciser kicking his or her legs vigorously during this lift. Do each leg extension slowly without bouncing in and out of the fully extended leg position.

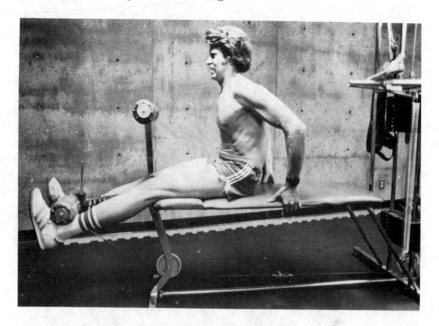

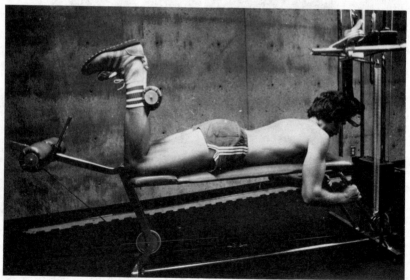

Leg curls. Reduce the weight from your leg extensions before beginning the curls.

In *rear* leg curls, you are working the complementary leg muscles. Leg curls work the hamstring muscle group. Go slowly and use less weight than you do on the front leg extension.

Dips: These are tough. It is all arms and back as you try to dip your entire body down before raising it back up. The dip is a good builder of arm and shoulder girdle muscle strength.

Dips.

Freestanding Weights

Freestanding weights come in all varieties, from Olympic competition weights to the home set ordered through a mail-order catalog. Because they present more possibilities for working muscle groups in various ways, freestanding weights are the body builder's choice.

In the free weight exercises shown below, follow these three basic lifting rules:

1. Use moderate amounts of weight (not so heavy that you strain excessively).
2. Try for the full range of motion when making each lift.
3. Breathe fully during each repetition.

Bench Press: This exercise is good for the chest and shoulder girdle muscles. Be sure to have someone spot you on this exercise. The spotter can take the weight out of your hands if it suddenly becomes too heavy or unwieldy.

Bench press with freestanding weights.

Bent Rows: This is a terrific exercise for the shoulder girdle muscles and one of the best weight exercises for cross-country skiers. Bring the weight up to your chest, then slowly let it back down. Bend your knees slightly to reduce the strain on your lower back.

Bent row position.

Upright Rows: This exercise works on the trapezius and deltoid muscles in the upper back. Bring the weight up to your chin and lower it back down. Notice the close hand grip.

Start of the upright row.

Finish of the upright row.

Power Cleans: Here is your chance to play Olympic lifter. Take it easy and don't put too much weight on the bar. Start each repetition with the bar close to your legs, thighs parallel to the ground, eyes up, and back straight. Initiate pull with the legs, not with the back.

The power clean.

Lateral and Front Dumbbell Raises: This is a fine lift routine to build the deltoids and create muscle balance.

The lateral dumbbell raise.

Other Weight Room Devices

Perhaps the most popular weight machine with professional athletes has been the Nautilus. A Nautilus machine works on variable resistance and reportedly isolates individual muscle groups better than any other type of weight training machine. If you have access to a Nautilus, consult with the trainer at the gym to find out which pieces of apparatus will help strengthen the muscle groups you use in cross-country skiing.

Working at Home

I find training at home more enjoyable than training in a gym. The atmosphere at home is more comfortable than any gym I've been to and you don't have those prying eyes peering at you as you grunt through another 60-pound bench press while the macho man next to you hoists 300 pounds as if it were a feather. At home you can put on some music, watch the news on television, or converse with a friend while getting in a good workout.

There are two types of home exercise that help with muscular development: device exercises and nondevice exercises. Device exercises rely on homemade or specially made devices that require some space. Work on these devices conditions specific muscle groups that are important to cross-country skiing. The nondevice exercises work on the same muscle groups but require little more than time, sweat, and strain.

A home exercise routine generally takes shape after a trial-and-error period during which you test all the available exercises and decide which you like best. Your home exercise program should be at least a half hour long to provide any training benefit. It's best to have a home exercise program mapped out during the summer since it will become the cornerstone of winter maintenance conditioning.

Devices

Exer-Genie: The Exer-Genie is a simple resistance device that is ideal for working on the diagonal stride poling motion. For best results the Exer-Genie should be placed high overhead so you pull down at an angle. The nylon webbing attachment strap and loop can be attached to a hook in the wall, to a tree limb, or to a fence (as shown in the photo) or laid over the top of a door and held in place by the shut door.

Once it is in place, set the resistance level on the Exer-Genie's tubular housing and pull on the individual straps to duplicate the diagonal stride poling motion. Pull until you feel a burning sensation in the triceps and latissimus dorsi muscles.

Pulling on an Exer-Genie.

Portability makes the Exer-Genie an ideal device to take along on a business trip or vacation to keep your muscles toned. The Exer-Genie is available from Exer-Genie, Inc., P.O. Box 3320, Fullerton, CA 92634. Ask for model EGS.

Arm Bands: Here is the homemade version of the Exer-Genie. Arm bands are made with two used 27-by-1¼ ten-speed bicycle inner tubes. After taking a chunk off each tube around the valve stem, tie the two tubes together to form one long tube. Hook or tie the tube overhead at the midpoint so that you have two tubes of equal length to pull on. Wrap the tube ends in your hands, back off until there is some resistance, and pull on the tubes to simulate the diagonal stride poling motion.

Arm bands are easily attached anywhere for a quick workout.

After practicing the poling, practice the double pole motion. Following this, turn so your back faces the point where the tube is attached and pull the tires out to a point in front of your chest for back and chest toning.

A derivation of the arm band is the leg band. A leg band is an uncut tire tube that can be wrapped around a post or pillar for leg exercises. After wrapping the tube around the stationary object, insert one ankle into the coils. The free leg is placed slightly ahead. You make a series of quick pulls up toward the lead leg with the leg in the tubing. This exercise builds quick-reacting quadricep muscles for the diagonal stride.

A doubled 27-by-1 inner tube makes a perfect leg band.

Incline Board: Easy to build out of plywood and two-by-fours, the incline board is perfect for sit-ups. Make sure your board is long enough, comfortably padded (with carpet remnants or ensolite), and that it has a wide soft strap to hold your feet in place.

Roller Board: In 1974 U.S. Nordic team coaches found a strange-looking piece of exercise apparatus in a Swedish sporting goods store. The device had been left behind by the East German national team following the '74 World Cross-Country Ski Championships at Falun, Sweden. Since the East Germans had done well in those championships, it was assumed that the device was at least partially responsible for their success.

The roller board: an easy-to-make home exercise device that is ideal for building upper body strength.

The device became known as the roller board. Basically a plywood ramp on which a skier pulls himself on a dolly, the roller board is a good device for the exercise skier and citizen racer who want to have a complete home workout facility. A roller board workout conditions the shoulder girdle muscle group.

To construct a roller board, take two ten-foot lengths of two-by-four and lay them on edge fourteen inches apart. Nail a piece of fourteen-inch-wide half-inch plywood onto the two-by-fours. This forms the ramp.

Two inches in from each edge, nail on two full-length one-by-two runners. The board is now complete except for a two-by-four crossmember that is nailed across the top of the board and tubular nylon straps that are attached to the ends of the crossbar.

On the dolly use either ½- or ¾-inch plywood (14 inches wide by 28 inches long) affixed with four nonswivelling dolly wheels. Set the wheels so they ride close to the one-by-two guide pieces on the ramp.

For best results with a roller board, set it at an angle at which you can easily pull yourself to the top. As you get stronger over a period of time, increase the angle and the number of repetitions of the exercise.

Total Gym: The Total Gym looks like a high-tech roller board. You can use it as a roller board and for other exercises. While a bit too expensive for most gymnasiums, the Total Gym is well worth the investment for people who would like a single device on which they can get a complete workout. For information on the Total Gym contact Total Medical Systems, 7730 Clairemont Blvd., San Diego, CA 92111.

Rowing Machines: Along with the stationary bicycles, rowing machines are becoming popular for home gymnasiums. Fifteen minutes of rowing is good total-body exercise. You work your arms, legs, back, and cardiovascular system during a good rowing workout. Two of the better rowing machines are the Tunturi and Dyna-Row 100. Both are sold at most reputable exercise equipment stores.

Pauls' Devices: Cross-country skier and inventor Ed Pauls has developed two exercise devices specifically for use by cross-country skiers. His skier's Upper Body Builder is a simple resistance device for use in simulating the single poling motion. The device attaches to the wall and takes up very little room.

His Nordic Track is the only readily available device on the American market that allows you to simulate the entire range of skiing motions. As you pull on an arm resistance device your legs go through a kick-and-glide cycle on a movable track. The track is attached to a flywheel that keeps the momentum going once you have initiated it with a few good kicks. Your feet are attached to the track by stirrups.

Information on these ingenious devices can be obtained by contacting Ed Pauls at PSI, 124 X Columbia Ct., Chaska, MN 55318.

Nondevice Exercises

Nondevice exercises are perfect for muscle toning. They are good for rainy day training at home or for a quick workout in your hotel room when you're on the road.

Sit-up/Crunchers: If you don't use an incline board for sit-ups, do them on the floor with bent knees. An extended version of the basic sit-up is the cruncher. Crunchers are very popular with body builders who want thin waists with strong, well-defined abdominal muscles. To do a cruncher, drape your legs over a bench or chair and make a series of quick forward sit-ups. Initiate the movement from your abdominal area. Don't curl up. Keep your arms at your side or across your chest.

Back Lifts: Get someone to hold your legs or anchor them with a strap to a bench or lock them under the edge of a bench for this exercise. Lift your body up and drop it back down just as in the Universal Gym exercise.

Calf Pack: Load a pack with some weight e.g., a flour sack or some books) and, standing with your face about three inches from the wall and your hands high above your head resting on

Drape your legs over a
bench or chair when you do
cruncher sit-ups.

(Below) Use a bench for
home back raisers.

the wall, lift one leg up behind the other. Now, with all your weight on one leg, dip down into a crouch, then spring up onto your toes. Repeat on one side until the leg gets tired, then switch legs.

Calf pack.

Chair Dips: This is the home equivalent of the dip station on the Universal Gym. Place two chairs shoulder width apart. Place the back of the palm of each hand on the front edge of each chair seat. With your legs extended out in front, resting on your heels, dip your body down using only your arms. This is good for the shoulder girdle and arm muscles.

Chair dip.

The Stationary Diagonal: When former cross-country great Martha Rockwell first introduced me to this exercise, I thought it was a little contrived. But over the years I have come to consider it one of the best home exercises for cross-country skiers. The exercise teaches people the rhythm of the diagonal stride and how to position their weight to one leg.

To do the stationary diagonal, start one leg and the opposite arm swinging as they would in the diagonal stride. Be sure to

Kick phase of the stationary diagonal.

Glide phase of the stationary diagonal.

get the opposite leg and arm going, not the arm and leg on the same side of the body. Relax and swing easily for two minutes, then switch to exercise the other arm and leg.

In the advanced version, rise up on your toes at the end of each rearward leg swing. Getting up on your toes helps your balance and your weight position and strengthens your calf muscles.

In the advanced stationary diagonal, you raise up on your toes on each rearward leg swing.

The Bomber: The final stage of stationary diagonal development is to make the movements explosive. The rearward kick is exaggerated so you come off your toes into the air. The forward leg swing becomes a forceful upward thrust into the air. The bomber is a pliometric exercise designed to train your muscles to react quickly. Bombers also get your heart pumping.

The rearward explosion of the bomber.

The forward lift of the bomber.

Aerobic Dancing: Many people have become involved in aerobic dance classes to get trim. Using exercises like the bomber, aerobic dancing is good low-level cardiovascular and muscular training. The beauty of this form of exercise is that it is done in a sociable group atmosphere. If you have attended such a class, use the same exercise in your home exercise routine.

The Circuit Course

The best way to combine cardiovascular and muscular conditioning is to set up a circuit course. A circuit training course is like a par course. Both have exercise stations interspersed along a running route. A typical circuit course might be three kilometers long with arbitrary exercises stations, or it might be a simple one-kilometer loop with one station at which all exercises are done.

A simple circuit course might include pushups, sit-ups and pull-up exercise stations. You run to the exercise station, do a set number of the exercise, and then run on to the next station. The more advanced course might include pulling on arm bands at one station, hill running at another, lifting a weight (a tree limb or a stone) at another, working out on a roller board, etc. It's all a question of how much time you have and how easy it is to lay out a circuit course close to your home.

4

Approximating On-Snow Activity

There are two exercises that most closely approximate on-snow techniques on dry land: roller skiing and hill running with poles.

Roller skis are simple devices with two rear wheels and, in the majority of cases, a ratcheted front wheel. The wheels are attached to an aluminum or laminated wood platform that is the width and thickness of a typical racing ski. With a binding installed on the platform, the skier is ready for summer road work.

On a backward push, the roller ski's ratcheted front wheel locks, giving the roller skier the feeling of a kick. When the roller skier drives the leg forward after the kick, all three wheels on the roller ski roll freely into a glide.

There is some controversy over the value of roller skis for training. All top international cross-country racers use them in their training, but it's how they use them that causes the controversy. Most Europeans use roller skis only to practice the double pole and kick double pole techniques. American skiers practice all phases of technique on roller skis in longer workouts.

There are three problems exercise skiers and citizen racers face with roller skis. First, they are expensive ($135 to $190). Second, a good roller ski workout may take time, much like a good ski workout. You normally have to travel to a good rolling section of road where traffic and gravel are minimal and the surface is soft enough for your poles to get sufficient grip. Third, there's a problem with poor technique habits that can easily be picked up from roller skiing.

The most common technique fault picked up from roller skiing is called the late kick. This simply means that the kicking leg rests too long on the ground before it is kicked. In proper diagonal stride technique, the kicking leg should be pushing backward as the skier's weight begins to shift onto the gliding leg. Because of the excellent grip on the roller skis (like having perfect wax), roller skiers tend to get lazy and kick later than they should.

A problem also exists with the weight of most roller skis. Because they are heavy and take a bit to kick back, many roller skiers lift their leg up at the end of their kick instead of letting the leg extend naturally to the rear. This is called "bicycling" the leg and translates to poor on-snow technique. As a result they get the late kick. In addition, the fear of falling on one's nose on the concrete also makes many roller skiers sit too far

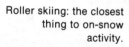

Roller skiing: the closest thing to on-snow activity.

back, with their center of gravity behind the lead foot instead of in front of it. Compounded, these problems leave many roller skiers with poor body positions and kicks that are carried over onto the snow where it takes time to correct them.

Top skiers generally diagonal stride only on steep or long, gently sloping uphills and use coaching and film analysis to make sure they aren't picking up bad technique habits. On the flats and gradual uphills, the top skiers double pole and kick double pole.

Roller skiing is difficult when compared to on-snow skiing. Roller skis tend to wander all over the road. You may be as stable as a rock on snow, only to become a wobbling spastic on roller skis. There's also a danger factor. A fall onto the asphalt or concrete, into the gutter or into a roadside hedge seems to be a part of the roller ski game.

If you intend to use roller skis in your training, stick to gentle terrain and double pole and kick double pole practice. If you have access to good coaching, try the diagonal, but only under your coach's supervision. If your time is limited and you want to do something that requires no special gear or capital investment, then stick to running and look for your cross-country specificity in other forms of exercise.

Hill Work with/without Poles

Hill workouts with and without poles are very specific and can often be done close to home. Hill workouts help develop an important part of ski technique while exercising the entire body and the cardiovascular system.

Earlier we discussed ski walking as one form of cardivascular conditioning. The next step up from ski walking is hill running without poles. The object is to drive up the hill with each leg and arm motion. Don't bound up the hill like a deer; rather, drive up the hill in a smoother, lower trajectory. Keep your head and eyes focused on the trail fifteen to twenty feet ahead.

After mastering a good hill running technique, take your

Hill running without poles: drive up the hill with the forward leg and arm.

Good hill running form: eyes up, energy directed up the hill.

poles along on a hill workout. Start by walking up the exercise hill several times to get the feeling of having your poles in your hands. You will immediately notice how the poles give you added thrust up the hill. When you begin running the hill with poles, concentrate on making firm pole plants and following through with a push-off and a short quick pole release at the end of each complete poling motion.

Marty Hall, former coach of the U.S. cross-country team, demonstrates hill walking with poles.

Hill workouts are interval workouts. Find a short hill course and run it several times. Check your pulse rate after you jog back down from the top of the hill to begin another run up. As soon as your pulse rate fails to drop back below 120, terminate the workout.

Hill running with poles.

5

Stretching and Flexibility

A workout is not complete without some flexibility and stretching exercises. Stretching is important for muscle resiliency. Recent studies indicate that many injuries are associated with stretching cold muscles. Therefore, it is advisable to warm up (jog or bicycle) for ten minutes before doing preworkout stretches. Be sure to try to end each workout with some stretching.

Stretch muscles slowly. Do not bounce into and out of each stretch position. Get into the stretched position slowly, hold the position for thirty or more seconds, then slowly come back out of it. The most flagrant example of bouncing (ballistic) stretching is people bobbing up and down as they touch their toes. Bouncing into a stretched position can tear muscles rather than stretch them. Here are some recommended stretches.

Toe Touches: This exercise stretches the hamstring and lower back muscles. Go slowly and let the muscles stretch out over a period of time. Don't lock your knees.

Calf Stretch: This is required for pre- and postrunning workout flexibility. Push against a wall, car, or fence and stretch the calf muscles slowly.

Calf stretches: important before and after a run.

Leg Over: Cross one leg over the other and twist your upper body in the opposite direction. This exercise stretches the hip area and the upper torso.

Leg over.

Trunk Extension: Sit with your legs directly in front of you and slowly reach forward to touch your ankles. As you loosen up, reach farther toward your toes. Work on calves, the lower back, and the hamstrings.

Trunk extension.

Shoulder Rotations: Slowly rotate your arms forward and then in reverse—good for loosening up the shoulder girdle muscles.

Shoulder rotations.

Side Bends: Clasp your hands overhead with your feet spread apart, bend to one side and hold the position, then raise body; bend to the opposite side. This is great for the muscles in the lower trunk.

Side bends.

Back Bends: A derivation of the side bend is the back bend. Place one foot about two feet behind your body. With your hands clasped overhead, lean as far back as possible. Alternate the rear foot. This exercise stretches the abdominals and the thigh muscles nicely and works on lower back muscles.

Back bends.

Cobra: This exaggerated arching of the back is excellent for stretching the abdominals and the neck and hyperextending the lower back.

The cobra.

Back Stretchers: If you have lower-back problems, like sciatica, these exercises are a must. Lie flat on your back and raise both knees. Raise one leg to your chest while the other remains straight out on the floor. Be sure to keep your back flat against the floor throughout these movements.

Stretch before and after workouts, remembering to warm up before your preworkout stretching. Try to stretch periodically during the day. If you can't get in enough stretching on a regular basis, devote one of your workouts to nothing but stretching.

Two good back stretchers.

6

Scheduling

Considering the variety of dry-land training resources available to cross-country skiers, putting together a good week-by-week training schedule shouldn't be too difficult. Unfortunately, most people find putting a schedule together and sticking to it the most difficult part of training.

To ensure a successful training program:

1. Block out enough time for a good workout on your training days.
2. Make your schedule flexible enough so you can miss a day and not lose ground.
3. Don't be compulsive and start training as if your future depended on being the equal of an Olympic athlete.

Schedule your training so that it fits easily into your daily routine. Select varied and enjoyable training activities. Train; don't strain. Use the hard day/easy day training approach. On your hard day, push yourself; on your easy day, relax with a more leisurely workout.

Training for the Advanced Ski Tourer

If your goal is to be more fit this winter so that each ski tour is more enjoyable, get into a three-day-a-week training schedule. With a three-day-a-week schedule, each training day is a hard day, each day off is an easy day.

Your goal in this program is to build cardiovascular endurance and muscle tone. The lack of proper cardiovascular conditioning prevents most ski tourers from becoming better cross-country ski technicians. If better technique is important to you, work on developing your cardiovascular system during the April-to-November period.

Month by Month

April: LSD workouts (running, bicycling, stationary cycling) for a half hour three times per week.

May: Same.

June: Same LSD workouts mixed in with other sports (canoeing, bouldering, kayaking, etc.) that help develop some upper body strength.

July: A mix of LSD workouts, sports for the upper body, and at least two natural interval runs.

August: More natural interval runs; begin to work on a home exercise routine. Increase workout duration to forty-five minutes when possible.

September: Same.

October: Stay with natural interval runs and try to make your home exercise routine more specific (roller board, Exer-Genie, arm bands).

November: Same.

Training for Exercise Skiing

People who ski for exercise tend to be active runners, cyclists, or tennis players during the summer. If you fall into this group, you probably need to refine some training skills so that your workouts have more effect on your cross-country skiing. Four days a week is plenty of time to carry out a decent training program that will prepare you for a winter of better skiing.

Try to develop greater cardiovascular endurance, better heart rate recovery, and more specific muscle strength and endurance. All of these elements will help you become a better skier.

Month by Month

April: LSD workouts and home exercise program (general strength and stretching); thirty to forty-five minutes per workout.

May: Same program with an occasional natural interval run.

June: Now is the time for work in other sports that help your strength and cardiovascular development while continuing your natural interval runs.

July: More of the same. Try to increase workout time to forty-five minutes with an occasional hour-long workout.

August: Begin working on a specific home exercise routine with emphasis on the Exer-Genie, roller board, arm bands, etc. Continue natural interval runs and general conditioning sports.

September: More of the same.

October: Now is the time to do some hill workouts with and without poles, to develop a circuit course, and to do pure interval runs.

November: Be specific—hill running, circuit course, home exercises. Do more natural interval and pure interval runs.

Training for Citizen Racing

I am of the opinion that in order to become a good citizen racer you should have some background in ski touring and exercise skiing. The most amusing examples of people who don't believe in this are top-level competitive runners. The better the runners, the more they think they can go out on the snow without any skiing background and win a citizen race. It seldom happens. Skiing techniques take time to develop and, at the citizen racer level of competition, having a good set of lungs and legs isn't enough.

Most citizen racers I know have a background in tour or exercise skiing. They are also competitive in other sports and tend to be compulsive trainers. Five days a week of training is enough for anyone. According to Per Olof Astrand, the father of modern physiology, when you are in shape you only have to train three days per week to maintain a high level of fitness. But to keep the compulsives happy, I will recommend five days a week of training. If you are active in running or bicycling competition, you might consider four days per week, allowing for rest days before and after each competition you enter.

As a citizen racer your goal is building a solid base of conditioning that will carry you through the ski season. To accomplish this, you must work on cardiovascular endurance and muscular strength.

Month by Month

April: If you raced during the preceding ski season, take two or three weeks off to allow your body to rest before starting on a new program. The rest gives the body and mind much needed vacations from the rigors of competition, and it allows you to change your mental set for the spring and summer training period ahead. After the rest, start off your training with LSD runs and an easy home exercise routine.

May: LSD and natural intervals; begin to become more specific in your home exercise routine. Do workouts of one hour.

June: The same cardiovascular and home exercise program, plus sports that work on the upper body. Start weight training to build strength.

July: Natural interval runs, upper body sports, hill running and roller skiing, and weights; workouts of one to one and a half hours.

August: Same.

September: Same as before; add some spice to the workout routine with pure interval runs and work on the circuit courses.

October: Same as above; begin home exercise work on specific muscle groups with the Exer-Genie, roller board, and arm bands. As you switch over to home exercise with these devices, cut back on your Universal and freestanding weight workouts. Cut workout duration to one hour.

November: This is the month to add your pure intervals, plus natural interval runs, hill running, home specific exercises, and an occasional roller ski.

The Training Log

Keeping track of your training activities in a logbook can be very beneficial. Entries in the book can be as lengthy or as brief as you desire. Generally it's good to note your pulse rate before the workout, the type and duration of the workout, and your pre-, during, and postworkout feelings. Here is a typical log entry: "Pulse sixty-five. Ran eight miles over hilly terrain at eight minutes per mile. Felt sluggish before the run, but after the first two miles started to feel like a tiger. Feeling good at this writing, two hours after the run."

The logbook serves a dual purpose: it is a record of the training you do during a period of time and of your mental and physical states during that training. Many skiers use their logbook later in the season to help them determine why they were successful or unsuccessful that season. A typical example might be the skier whose upper body tired easily during the season, costing him several important victories. Checking back over his logbook, he finds he did too much running during his dry-land training and not enough strength work. Proper use of the logbook allows the training athlete a chance to see the whole picture and balance out his or her training whenever necessary.

In tracking your mental and physical states, the logbook is

equally valuable. Over a period of time you will see how your log entries can give you clues as to when and how not to train. Recurring feelings that affected a day's training for better or for worse will begin to show up. Going back over a logbook, top skiers begin to understand their body and mind better and to heed the warnings they give the athlete.

Try keeping a training logbook or diary and see if it is helpful to you in laying out a training schedule and learning to listen to your body.

Listening to Your Body

The training logbook is the orderly way of beginning to learn about your body. The more spontaneous way is to learn to appreciate signals your body gives you. Earlier we talked about the importance of pulse rates and how an inordinately high resting rate was a good indicator of stress or approaching sickness. There's more to it than pulse, however. There are those small clues you will begin to pick up as you get involved in training that help you learn about how your body functions and when it is saying "go" and when it is saying "whoa."

Today we are deluged with hypothetical information from running magazines on the values of training. Training to these specialty publications is a panacea for all our problems and physical ailments. Not true. While some people may feel good training on days after they have endured a lot of mental strain, others might undergo a negative reaction and the stress of training may add to that under which they are already laboring. There are no absolutes to training. How you feel and what your body is telling *you* are more important than any of the easy answers you read about in magazines.

7

Diet and Health

It's useless to get involved in a training program if you continue to smoke a pack of cigarettes a day and eat junk food. The good training effect gained from exercise can be dulled through poor health habits and poor nutrition. Smoking is out if you want to train. Rest is important. Eating well is important.

You must eat well to stay well during training. There is a commonly held myth that if you are in training you can eat what you like from America's bountiful junk food table and survive nicely. Not so. While this might be remotely possible for a top young athlete who can get enough nourishment from sawdust burgers and french fries, the average person in training has to watch his or her food intake and start to eat right.

Eating right means many things to many people. Just as there are fitness fanatics who say that exercise means everything, so there are food fanatics who declare that good food is everything. I will take a moderate stance in between the two groups. A combination of good food, healthy exercise, and intellectual stimulation builds a better person.

Without dipping too deeply into nutrition, let me set out a

basic diet that will be very helpful to you in training. Take at least 70 percent of your foods in the form of complex carbohydrates (potatoes, beans, vegetables, whole grains) with the other thirty percent divided evenly between fats and protein. Carbohydrates turn rapidly into sugar that is stored in the muscles as glycogen. Glycogen is the energy source on which our muscles rely in training and competition. You have probably heard of athletes "hitting the wall." Well, this often happens when their muscles run out of glycogen stores.

In addition to the 70 percent carbohydrates rule, you should consider taking in a good part of your carbohydrates in raw form. When bicyclist John Marino set the transcontinental cycling record in 1980 (twelve days and three hours) he did so on a high-carbohydrate diet, 70 percent of which was raw food.

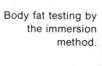

Body fat testing by the immersion method.

You are what you eat, and if you are eating mostly complex carbohydrates, avoiding sugars, and starting to cut down on your meat consumption, you are on your way to better health and better training days.

Body Composition

A few years ago only the top athletes had access to testing facilities where they could learn more about their body composition and how much stress they could take during training. Today many fitness clinics offer these services to the general public.

The body fat composition and stress test offered by fitness clinics and sports medicine facilities should be taken by anyone getting involved in a ski training program. The submaximal stress test is conducted on a stationary bicycle. It determines your training rate, heart rate, your heart rate recovery level, and your overall fitness level compared with those of your peers.

The body fat test is done in a tank of water. It reveals how much lean body mass (bone and muscle) and how much fat you have. This test can be a shocker. I've seen svelte model-type women who turned out to have extremely high body fat content. The reason: they are inactive and have no muscle fiber. While staying trim with diets, they have let their muscles atrophy. If you let your muscles go to waste, your body becomes fat even though you may look trim.

If a man has more than 15 percent body fat and a woman more than 20 percent, they need to go to work on themselves. The secret to getting below the recommended percentage levels is not dieting, but exercise. Throw out the bathroom scales and the diet books as your first muscle toning exercises. A combination of good food and exercise will lower body fat.

Anyone who is taking up training for cross-country skiing should take a submaximal stress and body fat test three times a year. The tests give you an indication of the positive effects of your training program, and they reaffirm the fact that you are doing your body some good by training.

8

Winter—It's Tough to Get Started Again

Every year I devise a plan to arrive on snow in such magnificent condition that skiing will be a breeze from the moment my skis are put into the track. But every year I'm amazed at how demanding cross-country skiing really is during the first few agonizing days back on skis. Day one on snow is given over to grumbling and the maintenance of minor gear problems. Then, with all the gear in order, I suffer the trials and tribulations of crossed tips, poorly waxed skis, and poles that seem to go everywhere but where I want them to go. Heaven forbid that I try a skate or step turn.

On day two the confidence is up. I charge off, skiing like a demon. All that bicycle training, running, kayaking, and roller skiing will make this easy, I think. No, it won't. I find out soon enough that it's going to be tough getting used to cross-country skiing again as I wipe my sweat-soaked brow and gasp for air.

There are few certainties in this life. But I'm here to report that no matter how good an off-season training program you have followed, those first few days back on snow are tough and depressing. Nirvana is putting on your skis for the first time at

the beginning of a season and skiing like you did at the end of the previous season.

Wintertime is maintenance time. The base of conditioning developed during the off-season is not enhanced but is maintained. Your winter fitness goal is to ski as often as possible. To maintain a good level of conditioning throughout the winter, you will need just a few hours of light training during the week and longer skiing sessions on weekends.

Finding enough time to train during the week is a greater problem in winter than in summer. The days are short and cold. Unfortunately, there are far too few lighted ski and running trails in North America where people can work out during winter evenings. Without lighted trails, you have to be creative in developing a conditioning maintenance program that fits into your daily schedule and doesn't become too boring.

Maintenance Training

The weekend becomes the focus for your winter training. On Saturday and Sunday you have the opportunity to fine-tune your skiing skills and prepare your body for touring, exercise skiing, or citizen racing. During the week training is low-key, consisting mainly of home exercises and basic cardiovascular workouts.

For best results during the week, try to get in four light workouts: two that work on cardiovascular conditioning and two that work on general muscle toning. The workouts should last from thirty to sixty minutes. Specific muscle groups will get plenty of activity on weekends while you are skiing, so concentrate on stretching and more general exercise routines during the week.

Two days of running should be sufficient for cardiovascular conditioning. Natural interval runs are your best bet. If running on dark icy streets doesn't appeal to you, try running on an indoor track or take up stationary cycling or swimming. I mix in running with stationary cycling. My personal stationary ride consists of fifteen minutes before work while watching one of the early morning shows on television and thirty minutes in the evening while watching the news.

For overall muscle fitness, start each workout with a light jog (around the block or in place), then stretch and start your exercise routine. A typical hour-long workout might include bent knee sit-ups, back lifts, calf packs, chair dips, pulling on an Exer-Genie, using the roller board, and some stationary diagonaling. After completing the exercise routine, do some additional stretches before quitting.

On Snow

The earlier you get onto snow, the better. You may have had an excellent dry-land training season, but if you don't put in any time on skis, even the best dry-land training effort will not make you a better skier.

One of the most common mistakes skiers make when they first get onto snow is going too fast too soon. Early in the season, try to rein in your enthusiasm. Go slow and long. Give yourself a chance to get your skiing back into a groove. The longer you ski at a slower pace, the more you will work on technical refinements. You want to get your technique down early in the season so you don't have to waste time and energy making technique adjustments all winter long. Going out and flailing around a ski track as fast as you can early in the season will only make your skiing technique sloppy.

Another reason for going slow is your health. Too many skiers have developed colds and bronchial problems from going too hard too soon without adjusting slowly to the rigors of skiing and to the cold air. Train long and slow to begin with and save yourself for a long ski season.

Long and slow means skiing for a set period of time, not for a set distance, at the lower end of your training level pulse rate. Slowly increase your tempo and vary it and the length of your workouts as the season progresses.

Exercise skiing for fun and better health.

As you progress and feel more comfortable on skis, the time will come when you will want to begin concentrating on what you want to get out of your skiing during the remainder of the ski season. If you are an advanced ski tourer, your main goal should be to ski better longer. You should want to be able to make long tours in less time and feel stronger throughout the length of the tour. You know your training has been successful when you can ski all day and still have enough energy to ski well over the last kilometers of a long tour.

If you are an exercise skier, you should want to ski better longer, just like the advanced ski tourer. The result of your spring-through-fall training program should make every day of prepared track skiing more exciting. The difference between your skiing before and your skiing after you began training will be better technique, increased strength, and the ability to do things on skis that you once thought impossible. Good physical conditioning will translate into more powerful, graceful technique and increased endurance that will allow you to maintain that technique for extended periods over more difficult terrain.

The citizen racer will have better technique, more stamina, and better results after training. Most citizen racers do not have strong conditioning backgrounds, even though they may have excellent technique. A racer may have all the technique in the world and a great deal of enthusiasm, but that won't help him when he's twenty-seven kilometers out in a thirty-kilometer race and his legs begin to wobble, his head spins, and his lungs feel as if they're on fire.

For most citizen racers a race begins with an energy-sapping, flailing getaway. With whatever energy he has left, the racer goes all out trying to keep up with the race leaders. In between long stretches of flailing, the racer might ski smoothly for a few seconds. But these moments are few, and soon our racer drags himself over the finish line and falls into an exhausted heap.

As a well-trained citizen racer, you will find that races become more enjoyable and rewarding. You feel in control at the start, you pace better throughout the race, and you finish with a strong surge. When the race is over you recover within minutes instead of days.

9

Training for Racing

There are many different ways to look at racing. For some people racing is a social occasion; for others it is a test of their will and a chance to see how they perform against other people in their age group. Many people race at a leisurely pace; others ski fast and use up every ounce of their energy. Every racer likes the feeling of accomplishment that comes from having skied the distance and finished. There is room for racers of every ability and outlook in cross-country skiing.

Just as there are differences in people's ideas about racing, there are also differences in what people think a distance race is. For some, any distance is akin to a marathon race; for others, any race under thirty kilometers is considered short. Generally, short races are five to ten kilometers long; the longer marathon races could be considered anything from twenty to sixty kilometers.

Two years ago a magazine editor told me that he was training hard for a ski marathon. "How long is the race?" I asked. "Ten kilometers," he replied. Ten kilometers never struck me as a marathon distance, but when I considered how long the editor had been skiing and the amount of free time he had to train in, I was more appreciative of his effort and the fact that for him ten kilometers was indeed a marathon race.

Ten kilometers has become a very popular foot running distance and it is becoming more popular with cross-country ski race organizers. Thousands of people may ski and run the marathon distances, but many more thousands compete at the shorter distances like five and ten kilometers.

Ten-Kilometer and Shorter Races

A typical ten-kilometer cross-country citizen race will be won in thirty-five to forty minutes with the last stragglers crossing the finish line in just over an hour. For the skiers in the front of the pack, the race is almost entirely anaerobic activity. From the fast sprint at the start to the last surge before the finish, the lead racers go at top speed. It's as if they are doing a prolonged interval workout. There is very little time to slow down and stretch out your skiing when you compete to win at distances of ten kilometers or less. If you plan to race the

shorter distances, your training should be geared to preparing yourself for short periods of hard work.

To excel at the shorter distances, be sure to include interval and tempo workouts in your weekly ski program. Intervals have been discussed at some length, but tempo training is a new term. Tempo training is skiing over a set distance at race pace. Both intervals and tempo workouts require a hard effort and too many of these workouts can break you down physically. Use caution in setting up your training program and don't overdo your interval or tempo training.

Interval workouts prepare you cardiovascularly and muscularly for the intense work of a shorter race. Vary your interval workouts to work on the different aspects of technique. One workout might be a series of intervals on an uphill section of track, another might be on a gently sloping downhill, and a third might be on a very slight uphill section. In each workout you are trying to perfect different aspects of technique while building cardiovascular strength.

On the uphill section workout, practice skiing smoothly into the base of the hill, shifting into a faster rhythm to ski up the hill, and finally pushing on over the top of the hill with an all-out effort. The important part of the drill is to pace yourself so as to have enough breath left near the top to push on over vigorously. Ski over the top of the hill on each repetition, turn around, ski back over and down, and repeat the interval as soon as your pulse rate drops below 120.

During a workout on gently sloping downhill terrain, you want to emphasize double poling technique and the kick double pole. The object is to push hard over a short section of track, stop, turn around, and ski slowly back to start another interval. Interval workouts of this type help build strong, quick-reacting muscles in your back and arms and make your cardiovascular system better adapted to the rigors of short races.

On a gentle sloping uphill workout, diagonal stride along the section of track at as high a rate of speed as possible. This workout will help you learn to maintain your technique at a faster tempo without having it fall apart.

Do an easy warm-up ski and some stretching before each interval workout. If you do an interval workout on Saturday, ski longer and easier on Sunday. Never stray too far from the hard/easy approach to training.

Intervals are hard work and many people hate them. The alternative is the tempo workout. In a tempo workout you might ski the same distance as you will race in an upcoming event. Say you have a five-kilometer race coming up in two weeks. Two Saturdays before the race you might ski five kilometers at race pace to train your body and mind for the rigors of the upcoming race.

It is best to combine tempo and interval workouts in your winter training effort. But, if intervals are not to your liking, try to ski a good tempo workout every other week until you get into the actual race schedule.

Long-Distance Racing

Long-distance ski racing requires a different mental set and training regimen. The best way to train for longer races is to put in time on your skis. Ski long and slow during most of your workouts, extending the length of time of each workout as the season progresses. Use shorter (twenty kilometers and less) natural interval ski workouts for training variety. Inject an occasional interval workout to keep yourself in top shape.

The long slow ski workouts are needed to get your muscles used to working efficiently over long periods of time. You will notice that as you train at long distance your cardiovascular system is not taxed so greatly. What are taxed are the muscle groups that are called on to work over and over again for an extended period of time.

Mental preparation is as important as any other aspect of long-distance ski training. It is very easy to ski for an hour without losing your concentration. But try skiing for two, four, or even seven hours without losing your concentration and your will to go on. It is very difficult. In long-distance ski racing you have to concentrate and you have to learn to work through and

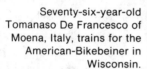

Seventy-six-year-old Tomanaso De Francesco of Moena, Italy, trains for the American-Bikebeiner in Wisconsin.

fight off the momentary depressions that make you want to quit.

By skiing longer distances in your training, you become more aware of the mental problems you will encounter during a long race. One minute you will be sailing along feeling fine only to suddenly feel rotten. You let up for a microsecond and your ski tips cross, sending you on your nose. That easy uphill suddenly looks like the side of Mt. Everest after forty-five kilometers, and that short, easy downhill becomes the walls of the Grand Canyon as you begin to lose your mental and physical energy.

There is another aspect of long-distance training that is too often overlooked. This is learning how to eat during a race to keep your energy resources from becoming depleted. A long race requires lots of fuel, and the smart ski marathoner learns to eat well before the race and to eat and drink as much and as often as possible during the race.

We will get into prerace and in-race eating later on, but it is important to note now that you should practice with prerace diets and in-race feeding along with your other forms of distance training. Only with practice will you learn which foods work in your prerace diet and which foods give you energy during a race.

Long-distance ski racing may be the most demanding individual competition. Do not go into a long-distance race unprepared. I tried it, and from the day after my first disastrous long-distance race, I have gone into my marathon races well prepared. If you are physically fit and mentally ready, the long-distance race is a joy to ski. It's a race of tactics and the opponent is yourself. It's not whether you win or lose; it's how you eat before the race, how you pace yourself, how you eat during the race, and how well you keep yourself together mentally that counts.

Distances, Distances

There are no set distance requirements for cross-country citizen races. Five- and ten-kilometer races are considered sprints by many racers; anything between fifteen and thirty kilometers is generally classified as middle distance; and marathons are anything over fifty kilometers.

A lot of the older traditional cross-country races are run at distances that coincide more with good logistical start and finish points than with some grand decree handed down by the powers of skiing. Oregon's John Craig Memorial Race, as an example, is twenty-four kilometers long one year, eighteen the next, and may be longer or shorter the year after, depending on how much snow is left on the McKenzie Pass Highway. Wisconsin's Otter Run is billed as a twenty-four kilometer race but skis like a twenty-kilometer race. But who cares? It's long enough when it is 15° F. and the finish line means the warmth of the Birkensee Resort, food, and beer.

Olympic distances are 5 and 10 kilometers for women (with the addition of 20 kilometers for the '84 Olympic Games) and 15, 30, and 50 kilometers for the men. The famous Euroloppet series of marathon races in Europe includes races of 75 and 85 kilometers. Most of the Great American Ski Chase marathon races are 50 kilometers with one 60-kilometer race (the American Ski Marathon in Vermont) and one 100-kilometer race (50 kilometers per day—the Minnesota/Finlandia).

Distances are deceiving. A ten-kilometer race can seem like a fifty-kilometer race when the snow is slow and the waxing is difficult. An icy fifty-kilometer race may seem to fly by as fast as a ten-kilometer race. As with all things in cross-country racing, snow and wax are still the big factors in how tough or easy a race is.

Suggested Race Training Schedule

November: If you are lucky enough to get onto the snow in November, use the time to get your skiing back into a groove. Ski long and slow for a set period of time, not for a set distance.

December:
Training for Short-Distance Racing
    Weekends: Long slow steady distance (one hour per ski session)

    Weekdays: Home exercise, two days; *Cardiovascular workouts, two days (workout duration: one half hour minimum)

Continue the above schedule for the first two weeks of the month, then follow this program:

    Weekends: Natural interval ski, one day (fifteen kilometers; interval or tempo workout the next day)

Training for Ski Marathons
Long slow distance skiing (up to two hours per session)
Rollerboard, Exer-Genie, exercises, two days; natural*
    interval runs, two days (workout duration: two
    hours)

Continue the above schedule for the first two weeks of the month, then follow this program:

Long two and one-half to three-hour ski, one day
Hour-long natural interval ski the next day

Use the same schedule as the first two weeks for in-week training.

January: Use the late December schedule with this warning: if you start to get bored, vary your routine. This means changing your home exercise routine by adding and deleting exercises. It also means skiing different distances, ski touring for fun, and going downhill skiing for a change of pace. Keep your program varied and interesting and you will have better race results.

Feburary/March: This is the heart of the race season in most areas of the country. If you plan to race every weekend or twice a month, cut back on your training and go all out in your racing. You cannot gain any extra strength during the week before a race. Rest and relaxation will help you more in the late season than compulsive training.

---

*Insert roller ski workouts (double poling/kick double pole) and hill running with poles for foot runs whenever you can.

10

Before and During the Race

The Week Leading up to a Race

There are probably as many theories as to what to do during the week before a race as there are theories on what to do while in a race. Since most citizen races take place on Saturdays, I suggest doing a hard workout on the Saturday before and then tapering training off throughout the week leading up to the race day. For the short-distance racer, the hard workout the week before the race should be a tempo workout. For the marathon skier the hard workout should consist of a two- to three-hour ski at a moderate pace. Practically speaking, these workouts give you an idea of what to expect in your upcoming race, and they tire you out so you don't get too compulsive and try to do some catch-up training during the week.

During the six days before the race, stick to a schedule like this:

Sunday: Easy ski—45 minutes
Monday: Easy home exercise routine (back lifts, sit-ups, etc.)—30 minutes

Tuesday: Cardiovascular workout (jog, swim, stationary cycle)—30 minutes
Wednesday: Exer-Genie/roller board—30 minutes
Thursday: Rest and relax
Friday: Rest and relax—maybe fifteen minutes of stretching after a short warm-up jog.

I cannot emphasize the importance of the last two days enough. Try to relax and get as much rest as you can. Since you may have to drive some distance to the race, plan ahead so that travel doesn't become mentally and physically draining. Drive to the race site the night before or early in the morning of the race and share the driving with other racers so you arrive fresh and ready to race.

Race Day

Every year citizen racers seem to get more stupid instead of smarter. They may train better, eat better, and wax better, only to arrive at a race twenty minutes before the start and

think they have allowed enough time to get ready to race. If you want to be at your best in a race, you have to get to the race site at least an hour before the start to make sure you and your equipment are functioning properly.

When you arrive, park and get all the equipment you will need out of the car. Register and get your bib. After registration, test the snow and begin your wax testing. Wax your skis and go out for an easy warm-up ski. Following the easy ski, return to your base of operations and do some stretching exercises like the ones shown in the photographs. Stretch slowly to get limber. After stretching, work on your final wax job.

Time is now getting short, and you have to make the last-minute preparations: touch up your wax job; go to the bathroom; get your bib on and tied securely; make sure your boot laces are tight; check the wrist straps on your poles, and make sure they are tight; and just before you ski to the starting area, take your warm-ups off and leave them in a safe place.

Before the start, ski easily for a few hundred yards and follow this with some quick short intervals to get your heart rate up.

Four prerace stretching exercises.

To relieve the most pressing prerace psychological barrier, try following these rules:

1. Trust your own waxing ability.
2. Don't ask what other people are waxing with and don't change your mind about your wax job five minutes before the race because you hear a top racer is using something else. Stick with what you have.
3. Carry along some waxes in a marathon race in case conditions change. In a short race, go with what you already have on the skis; it takes too much time to stop and rewax when you're racing for short periods of time.

11

Prerace Diet and In-Race Food and Drink

Perhaps you were brought up, as I was, with the idea that the steak-and-egg high-protein football-team diet was best for athletes. Not true. Research has proven that carbohydrates (carbs), not proteins, are the enduring athlete's best food friends. Our muscles rely on muscle sugar in the form of glycogen. Carbohydrates synthesize into glycogen ten times faster than proteins do.

In the late 1960s Swedish physiologists devised a carbohydrate diet for endurance athletes. A week before a major race a skier or marathon runner would do a long hard workout during which he would deplete the glycogen stores in his muscles. For three days after the workout, the athlete would eat 10 percent carbohydrates and 90 percent protein and fat. For the three days before the race the athlete would eat 90 percent carbohydrates and 10 percent protein.

The carbohydrate-loading diet was first tested on cross-country ski racers, but it ultimately found acceptance with marathon runners. Many runners experienced increased performance using the depletion/carbohydrate-loading diet. By the mid 1970s carb-loading was standard operational procedure for almost all marathon runners.

But, as more endurance athletes experimented with the depletion/carb-loading diet, more found fault with it. Most athletes complained of losing strength during the three days of high protein and fat consumption. This lack of strength might cause the athlete to curtail his training or become ill.

Today most world-class endurance athletes go through the hard workout phase of the diet plan, but they eat normally, with at least 70 percent of their foods being carbohydrates, for the six days leading up to the race. Try the following prerace diet plan for long-distance marathon ski racing.

1. A week before your marathon race, do a long hard workout.

2. Eat normally, with 70 percent of your foods being carbohydrates.

3. Try to eat bland foods that digest easily. This is particularly important the night before the big race.

4. *Don't* overload on carbohydrates. An overload can cause temporary increases in blood sugar levels that will alter muscle metabolism.

During the week before the big race competitors eat all sorts of carbohydrates, but the night before the big event they invariably eat pasta. Spaghetti is the most popular prerace meal and is the reason that Italian restaurants are jammed before major ski marathons.

Spaghetti is popular with good reason. It is bland and is easily digested. There are other foods that are higher in carbohydrates that you should also consider: beans, bulgur, oatmeal, and brown rice. Consult a reputable text on foods and come up with a varied menu of carbohydrates that will make your prerace-week eating more enjoyable.

Race Day Food

Let's say that you are skiing in a short race that starts at 10:00 in the morning. I would suggest a light meal (fluid, toast, and a piece of fruit) at 7:00. If the race is later in the day, eat a light breakfast about four hours before the competition.

It is better to eat light and ski on the meal you had the night before than to try to digest food as you ski along. Arriving at the starting line with food and drink sloshing around in your stomach spells trouble. The undigested food will inhibit your performance and will often make you ill.

Longer races require more food planning. On race day the marathon skier has to consider his in-race food and drink as carefully as his wax. The marathon skier can eat a fairly hearty meal four hours before the race. Pancakes and coffee are a popular premarathon meal.

In-Race Food and Drink for Marathoners

In most marathon ski races competitors begin to lose the glycogen stores in their muscles as the race wears on. If a racer has done a week of carbohydrate loading, his glycogen reserves will not be reduced as rapidly. If, however, he loses his glycogen reserves, he is most likely to "hit the wall."

I hit the wall with a resounding thud in the American Birkebeiner a few years ago. I followed a basic carbohydrate-

This shot was taken at the forty-kilometer point of the men's fifty-kilometer race at the 1979 Finnish Ski Championships.

loading plan the week prior to the race but failed to heed a coach's advice about eating often and early in the race. I skied past tables piled high with food and drink, thinking my carb-loading would carry me through the entire race. If I stopped, it was only for a few cups of liquid.

Halfway through the race I felt like a tiger. At the forty-kilometer mark I started to sag mentally and physically. At fifty kilometers, five kilometers from the finish, I passed out on the ski track. I simply ran out of gas (glycogen).

Even the best skiers fall apart when they "hit the wall."

In subsequent marathon races I have gone a bit overboard in eating and drinking heavily along the course. But I have finished every subsequent marathon and felt in all of them that I had something left over during the last five kilometers of the race. What the Birkebeiner experience taught me is that you have to eat and drink throughout a race to replenish your energy.

Drinking to replace lost fluids is important in a marathon race.

Now, to help myself along the way, if trouble hits between aid stations, I carry my own food supply in a fanny pack. Included are raisins, dates, and bread. Last year I started adding a cut-up banana and found it a great treat. If I feel the "wall" approaching, I swing my fanny pack around, open it, and eat some of my food as I glide over a gently sloping downhill section of track. I have known the food to work wonders when all seemed lost.

Every marathon racer should practice well in advance of the big race with prerace dieting and in-race feeding. You have to become familar with which foods agree with your system before the race and which foods pep you up during a race. You should also become familar with skiing with a fanny pack and taking foods out of it along the course.

What you drink during a race is equally important. Cross-country racers lose a great deal of fluid. The rule of thumb for liquid replacement is 250 milliliters of fluid for every fifteen minutes of activity. This is hard to do because aid stations are not spaced together very closely in races. My recommendation is to drink at least three cups of fluid at every aid station and take along half a liter of fluid in your fanny pack in case you begin to falter.

The ideal in-race drink is a simple solution of sugar and water. Two-percent sugar is considered the ideal amount. Anything more than 2 percent and the stomach has difficulty in emptying the fluid into the system so it can go about its replacement business. Some athletes use regular table sugar in water or add a small amount of concentrated drink that is heavy in sugar.

Replacement drinks like ERG, Gatorade, Body Punch, and XL-1 have been very popular, but recent research has proven they are basically useless. These drinks replace the salts the body loses during exercise. They do very little to replace the water you lose through sweat. Stick with either water or a simple sugar and water solution for best replacement results.

You can take your in-race drinks hot or cold. Cold drinks empty from the stomach faster than the hot ones. The time factor is important to international ski racing stars, but for citizen racers the time is insignificant. So, if a hot drink makes you feel better and revives your spirits, by all means take it.

The Caffeine Connection

A favorite drink of veteran marathon skiers and runners is coffee. Like so many people, I assumed for years that coffee was popular with the long-distance endurance athlete because it kept him awake and alert during the late stages of a race. What I subsequently discovered is that coffee serves a very valuable function in helping the endurance athlete's system draw on fat reserves for energy.

As we noted earlier, our muscles rely on muscle sugar (glycogen) for energy during endurance competition. When our glycogen reserves run low, we run the risk of "hitting the wall." Some time ago it was discovered that a chemical in our systems called epinephrine would stimulate the use of fat for energy. Caffeine simulates epinephrine and helps an athlete's system switch from using muscle glycogen stores for energy to using free fatty acids for energy. Since we all have fat to burn and, as a race wears on we want to preserve our glycogen stores, ingesting caffeine through coffee before and/or during a race has become very popular with endurance athletes.

I first recognized the importance of the caffeine connection during the seventy-five kilometer Finlandia race in Finland. During the late stages of the race I began to run out of gas. No matter what I ate, I could not revive my energy.

At the fifty-five kilometer point I started drinking coffee out of desperation rather than intelligence. It worked. I did not find a renewed source of energy, but I began to feel as though I was digging down and getting a boost from a hidden source in my body. As a result, I was able to finish the race in style and still have enough energy left to walk to my hotel.

It is important to note that the caffeine connection does more than help switch the body's cycle from a glycogen state to a free fatty acid cycle state. Caffeine also decreases perceived levels of exertion. In other words, you may be exhausted, but after a couple of cups of coffee at an aid station you feel as if part of your load has been lifted from your back.

Impressed with what caffeine will do for endurance athletes, the U.S. Nordic team began experimenting with time-released caffeine capsules. A capsule is taken by a racer before a long-distance race. About an hour and a half into the race, the capsule begins to work to switch the skier's system to a free fatty acid cycle.

Citizen racers don't have access to time-released caffeine capsules, so we have to rely on drinking coffee or one of the caffeine-loaded diet colas at an aid station during the race. If the races you plan to enter don't offer coffee at their aid stations, have someone meet you at a prescribed place on the course with your caffeine drink or carry your own drink along in a fanny pack.

I carry Tab that has been allowed to go flat. Tab has enough caffeine to start switching your system to a free fatty acid cycle. I put a half liter of Tab, cut slightly with water to eliminate the sugary taste, into my fanny pack and ingest the whole contents about three-fourths of the way through a long race.

Again, as with food, it is best to try coffee and colas during a long ski workout to see if they help you revive when your energy gets low. Some people have a natural aversion to caffeine and it makes them sick. Make sure caffeine agrees with your system before the race, not during the race when an upset stomach forces you to drop out.

When testing your personal caffeine drink (coffee or cola), try skiing for a set period of time (say, two hours) and then stop and drink coffee or a cola from a thermos laid along the track's side. Ski on for another forty-five minutes and see how the drink affects your performance. If the caffeine connection works for you, then try drinking your fluid from a bottle or small thermos stored in a fanny pack. Learn to swing the pack forward, open it, extract the thermos or bottle, and drink on the move.

12

Setting Reasonable Goals

No matter what your ability level is, it is always good to set a goal for yourself at the beginning of each ski season. Your goals will vary from season to season and should always be based on your personal perception of the sport and what you want from it. Do not get caught up in other people's expectations or the mythical universal expectations so often written about by coaches who see gold medals as the only goals in life.

Reasonable goals are ones like improving your time on a particular course, finishing a long marathon race, winning among your age group in a favorite race, skiing better and feeling better because you're in better shape. If you set a reasonable goal that requires work and dedication, you're on the right track. If, however, you set a goal that becomes all-consuming, you are headed for trouble or a great letdown. Setting too high a goal is often nothing but daydreaming or a way of setting yourself up for failure.

A few years ago I visted Finland's great cross-country skier, Juha Mieto. He told me that his goal had always been to be a world-class skier. He knew he had the temperament and the ability to get to the top, but early in his career he was hampered by rapid growth and awkwardness. "I told myself," the six-foot seven-inch 220-pound giant said, "to concentrate on my long-term goal. When other kids beat me as a junior, I would tell myself, 'Don't worry, you will catch them later.' I kept working and never lost sight of my goal."

Mieto's goals were reasonable and he kept working toward them. Blessed with tremendous strength and talent, the great Finn knew what he could eventually do and he did it. His persistence paid off just as yours will for you as a citizen racer if you set reasonable goals and work toward them over a period of time. Training your mind and body is the only way to reach your goals. In an endurance sport like cross-country skiing, there are no shortcuts or easy answers. You have to work hard for success.

This does not mean you should become totally immersed in cross-country skiing and competition. It means working toward a reasonable goal with a flexible, enjoyable training program. You should always view training and working for goals as a way of helping you get in touch with your body and your inner resources. Learning to tap your physical and mental resources through athletic training will help make your entire life more productive and more enjoyable.

Index